TONY PANG

Walking Wisdoms:
Father To Son: Sacred Wisdoms Passed Down Through African American Communities

M
G
MESAI GLOBAL

This book was professionally typeset on Reedsy.
Find out more at reedsy.com

Dedicated to the beautiful people of The Democratic Republic of the Congo

"The two closest things on earth are the teeth and the tongue, and even they sometimes get out of sync, and the teeth sometimes will bite the tongue, but they quickly get back on track and work together for the good of the whole." Bakongo wisdom passed down to Tony Pang from his Father

Contents

Preface

In the tapestry of existence, there are threads of wisdom woven by ancient cultures, whispered through generations, and carried across oceans. These threads, often hidden from the mainstream narratives, hold within them the profound secrets of the cosmos. This book, "Walking Wisdoms," is a journey into one such realm of wisdom, where the teachings of the Bakongo people, their Cosmogram, and their profound impact on diverse cultures are unveiled.

Imagine my father passing down wisdom to me, a timeless message that transcends generations. "Son," he says, "The two closest things on earth are the teeth and the tongue, and even those two get out of sync sometimes.

But this book is not just about a father's teachings; it's about the enduring wisdom of the Bakongo people, a vibrant and ancient culture whose influence stretches far beyond the borders of their homeland. It's about the Bakongo Cosmogram, a symbol that encapsulates a universe of knowledge, and how it has touched the lives of Native American communities. It's about the undeniable parallels between the Bakongo Cosmogram and the Native American Medicine Wheel, a testament to the interconnectedness of humanity's collective wisdom.

The story goes deeper as we delve into the powerful impact of Bakongo culture, religion, and the Cosmogram on African American communities in the United States. The Kongo cosmogram, introduced by enslaved Bakongo people during the trans-Atlantic slave trade, found a home in the hearts of Black Americans. It adorned the walls of church basements and was etched into pottery, a silent but potent reminder of heritage, resilience, and unity.

Yet, this book is more than an exploration of symbology and cultural exchange. It's a spotlight on history, revealing the rich tapestry of Bakongo culture and the enduring legacy of their cosmological wisdom. Ethnohistorical sources and material culture offer evidence of the Kongo cosmogram's existence before European contact and its continuous use in Central Africa into the twentieth century. This sacred symbol encapsulated the essence of the Kongo people, a metaphoric representation of their place within the cosmos.

As we embark on this journey, we must also acknowledge the shadows that mar the story. The Democratic Republic of Congo, a land with a painful history of conflict and ethnic cleansing, bears witness to the endurance of its people. This book is a call to shine a light on their plight, to remember the resilience of the human spirit even in the face of unimaginable suffering.

In "Walking Wisdoms," we unearth the ancient wisdom of the Bakongo people, illuminating the hidden corners of history, culture, and spirituality. It's a tapestry woven with love, unity, and the enduring search for meaning in the vast cosmos. May this exploration inspire you, dear reader, to seek deeper, to appreciate the threads that connect us all, and to cherish the secrets of the cosmos that lie within our shared humanity.

Acknowledgement

I'd like to start by thanking Allah (SWT), for giving me everything

I'd like to thank my Mom, who was the main inspiration behind this story. *"You are the wind beneath my wings"*

Thank you Kareemah for checking my grammar and giving the encouragement and support to keep me going.

Thank you, my lovely readers, you followed me and stayed with me.

Finally, I can't leave without expressing my gratitude to everyone over at JustWrite who made this book what it is today. I do not know what I would do without you guys!

If you enjoyed this story, then please be sure to show your appreciation by leaving a review on either Amazon or Goodreads. It would mean more than I can express!

Kongo Cosmogram

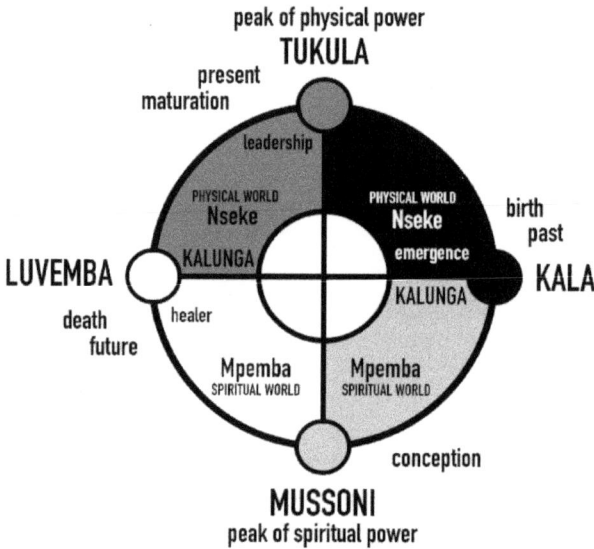

The Kongo Cosmogram was introduced in the Americas by enslaved Bakongo people in the trans-Atlantic slave trade. Archaeological findings in the United States show evidence that the symbol was honored by Black Americans, who drew the Kongo Cosmogram on the walls of church basements, as well as engraved it in pottery

Introduction

Menalik and Tin-sing strolled beneath the vast expanse of the night sky, stars winking like distant fireflies. The air was filled with a sense of anticipation, a question hanging in the air like a secret waiting to be unveiled.

Tin-sing couldn't contain his curiosity any longer. "Menalik," he began, "you've often spoken of universal wisdom, of teachings that seem to transcend borders and cultures. Can you share some of these with me? What are they, and where do they come from?"

Menalik paused, his eyes reflecting the wisdom of ages. "Son," he replied with a warm smile, "what you're asking about is the heartbeat of our shared human experience. It's the rhythm that connects us all, regardless of where we come from or the paths we tread. You see, this universal wisdom, these guiding lights, are like the whispers of the Creator sent down to all people in one form or another."

As they continued their leisurely walk, Menalik's words hung in the air, drawing Tin-sing closer to the heart of the matter. "To the Native Americans," Menalik continued, "it's the Red Road and the Medicine Wheel, a sacred circle that teaches balance, connection, and harmony with the world around us. It's a path to understanding and healing."

Tin-sing listened intently, intrigued by the notion of shared wisdom that spanned continents and cultures. "And what about our brothers in the east?" he inquired.

Menalik's eyes sparkled with the joy of sharing these profound insights. "Ah, to our brothers in the east, it's the Wheel of Life," he explained. "A representation of the continuous cycle of existence, reminding us of impermanence, karma, and the interconnectedness of all living things. It's a guide to living with purpose and compassion."

Tin-sing nodded, captivated by the beauty of these teachings. "And what of the Middle-East?" he asked.

Menalik's voice took on a deeper resonance. "In the Middle-East, my friend, it's the wellspring of Islam and Islamic Cosmology. It's a profound understanding of the divine order, a path to submission, and a reminder of the eternal connection between the Creator and creation. It guides hearts and souls toward enlightenment."

As they continued their journey, Menalik's words painted a tapestry of wisdom that transcended borders and boundaries. "And then," he said, "there's Africa, the cradle of humanity. Here, we find the Bakongo and the Kongo Cosmogram, a symbol that encapsulates the essence of existence within a circle. It's a reminder of our place within the cosmos, an embodiment of the eternal and the interconnected."

Tin-sing marveled at the vastness of these teachings, so beautifully different yet remarkably similar in their core messages. "So," he mused, "these are the secret universal wisdom you speak of?"

Menalik nodded, his gaze fixed on the horizon. "Indeed, my friend. These are the guiding stars that have illuminated the path for countless souls throughout history. They remind us that, no matter our journey, we are all bound by the same threads of existence, and the Creator's wisdom shines upon us all."

With that, they continued their walk beneath the celestial canopy, two friends connected not only by their conversation but by the timeless wisdom that transcended cultures, continents, and the very essence of their being.

The Creator

The stars shone brightly in the night sky as Menalik and Tin-sing sat on the porch, a gentle breeze rustling the leaves of the nearby trees. The conversation had turned to matters of the divine.

"Dad," Tin-sing began, "you've always told me about the Creator's guidance. Can you share more about it?"

Menalik's eyes held a serene wisdom as he spoke. "The Creator, my son, has made us all pure and clean. We are born with a soul untainted by the world. But when we venture out into this world, we're exposed to all its influences, some clean and pure, others muddy and foul."

. It's a reminder to steer clear of the muddy, dirty, and foul things that can taint our souls."

Tin-sing nodded, his gaze fixed on the night sky. "But what if we do get dirty along the way?"

Menalik smiled, his voice gentle. "Ah, my son, the Creator is merciful. When we falter and find ourselves covered in the muck of the world, the Creator has provided us with clean, pure water—water of prayer, love, and towels of redemption, hope, kindness, and tolerance."

He explained, "Just as we wash our bodies to cleanse away dirt, we can cleanse our souls with prayer and these towels of virtues. Redemption reminds us that we can always start anew, hope fuels our journey, kindness softens our hearts, and tolerance allows us to embrace others despite their flaws."

Tin-sing felt a profound sense of peace listening to his father's words. "It's like a spiritual bath for the soul."

Menalik nodded, his eyes twinkling with a deep understanding. "Precisely, my son. It's a way to purify ourselves and return to the Creator as pure as we were when we began our journey in this world."

Tin-sing couldn't help but ask, "Dad, have you ever felt a connection with the Creator?"

Menalik's gaze turned introspective. "Many times, my Son. In moments of solitude, in the beauty of nature, and in the love and kindness of others, I've felt the presence of the Creator. It's in those moments that I've found solace, guidance, and a profound sense of purpose."

Menalik smiled, his eyes alight with a wisdom born of a lifetime of contemplation. "Son, our connection to Allah is like no other. It's a bond beyond measure, deeper than the oceans, and vaster than the sky. But I've always felt that this connection could be even greater, richer."

Tin-Sing was curious, his eyes filled with wonder. "How, Dad?"

Menalik paused, choosing his words carefully. "You see, my dear son, many view Allah as a distant figure, someone to turn to only in moments of great need or when we're burdened by life's heaviest troubles. But imagine if we treated Allah as a constant companion, a best friend who walks with us every step of the way."

Tin-Sing's gaze fixed on his father, captivated by the idea. "A constant companion?"

Menalik nodded. "Yes, Tin-sing. Imagine if we shared not only our moments of sorrow and desperation but also our moments of joy, our laughter, and even our silliest thoughts. What if we spoke to Allah as we would to a cherished friend, openly and sincerely?"

Tin-Sing's eyes sparkled with understanding. "So, we should share everything with Allah? Our doubts, our questions, our happiness, and our fears?"

Menalik's voice was filled with warmth and affirmation. "Exactly, Tin-Sing. Allah is closer to us than our own jugular vein, as the Quran tells us.

We should turn to Him with all our concerns, large or small. Share your questions, your moments of uncertainty, and your musings about life. Feel the comfort in knowing that you're never alone in your thoughts."

Tin-Sing nodded, feeling a profound sense of connection. "I see, Father. It's like having a best friend who's always there, who understands us better than anyone."

Menalik's smile deepened. "Precisely, my son. And just as you'd turn to a best friend for advice, guidance, and comfort, you can turn to Allah with the same trust and love."

He shared a personal story. "I remember a time when I was facing a difficult decision. I sat in silence, seeking clarity, and suddenly, it was as if a gentle breeze whispered wisdom in my ear, guiding me towards the right path. It's moments like those that remind me of the Creator's love and guidance. Son, let's make salat"

As the night deepened, father and son sat in contemplative silence, enveloped by the mystery and wonder of the divine. It was a chapter of their journey together, exploring the profound relationship between the Creator and the human soul, a connection that transcended time and space.

Choosing a Mate

In the heart of the bustling city, Menalik and his son Tin-sing embarked on a walk that would weave together the wisdom of generations. The air was filled with the aroma of street food and the rhythm of life. Their conversation began with a topic that would shape Tin-sing's journey—choosing a mate.

"Dad," Tin-sing inquired, "how do you know when you've found the right person to share your life with?"

Menalik, with the wisdom of age and experience, smiled at his son's question. "Ah, choosing a mate, is one of life's most profound decisions. It's like picking a partner for a dance that will last a lifetime."

He continued, "First, you must recognize the importance of this choice. Your life partner will be your confidant, your companion through both stormy seas and tranquil waters. They will share in your dreams, your joys, and your sorrows."

Tin-sing nodded, absorbing his father's words. "But how do you make the right choice?"

Menalik's eyes twinkled as he spoke. "The key, my son, lies in shared values and spirituality. Look for a partner whose beliefs align with yours, someone who walks the same spiritual path. It's in this alignment that the foundation of a strong and enduring bond is laid."

He shared a bit of humor, recalling their earlier discussion. "And remember, Tin-sing, a little bit of humor goes a long way. If you are with a woman for six months or longer and you have never heard or smelled her fart, it might be a sign. Someone who can hide their farts for six months or more, who knows what else they can hide."

Tin-sing laughed, appreciating his father's light-hearted wisdom. "I'll keep that in mind, Dad."

"Don't forget the power of laughter. Look for a woman who loves to laugh and who has the ability to make you laugh. Life can throw some curveballs, but a partner who can lighten the mood and bring joy to your days is an incredible gift. Find someone who appreciates your sense of humor and shares her own—those are the moments that create lasting bonds."

He continued, "You see, love is a beautiful thing, but it's not enough on its own to sustain a lasting relationship. You need a strong foundation built on shared values and spirituality."

Tin-sing nodded, absorbing his father's words. "So, you mean we should look for someone who loves God more than they love us?"

Menalik smiled warmly. "Exactly, my son. When you find someone who loves God above all else, you can trust that their heart is in the right place. Their love for you will be guided by a higher purpose, and that's a love that can withstand life's storms."

Menalik continued, "Furthermore, don't underestimate the role of parents in this journey. No one knows and loves you better than your parents. Give them the opportunity to get to know your potential mate, to discern if this person is the right fit for you. Their blessings can be a guiding light."

As they strolled through the vibrant city streets, father and son discussed the profound significance of choosing a mate. Menalik understood that this decision would shape Tin-sing's life in ways he couldn't yet imagine. And Tin-sing, with his father's guidance, embarked on this journey with a heart filled with wisdom, humor, and the understanding that love and partnership were choices to be made with great care and consideration.

Relationships

As Menalik and Tin-sing continued their evening stroll. Their conversation drifted into the complex world of relationships.

"Dad," Tin-sing began, "I've seen couples who seem so perfect, and then they break up. Why is that?"

Menalik smiled knowingly. "Ah, relationships, my son. They're like the dance between your teeth and tongue. You see, the teeth and tongue work together every day, helping us chew our food and speak our words. But even they sometimes get out of sync."

Tin-sing raised an eyebrow, intrigued by his father's analogy. "How so?"

Menalik explained, "Well, sometimes your teeth might bite your tongue accidentally. It's painful, but it happens. But what's remarkable is how quickly they work it out and get right back to working together for the good of the whole."

Tin-sing nodded, starting to see the connection. "So, relationships have their ups and downs, just like teeth and tongue sometimes clash?"

"Exactly," Menalik confirmed. "No matter how close two people are, they're bound to face challenges. It's a natural part of being in a relationship. What matters is how they handle those challenges, how they communicate and work through them."

They continued walking, the city around them bustling with life. Menalik's eyes carried a depth of experience as he continued, "You asked about couples who seem perfect but break up. Well, sometimes, despite our best efforts, we can't change a person's character."

Tin-sing furrowed his brow, curious. "Why is that so hard?"

Menalik sighed softly. "Character is like the spots on a leopard's skin, my boy. You can't wash them away no matter how hard you try. People are who they are, and while love can be a powerful force, it can't fundamentally change someone's nature."

He paused, lost in thought for a moment. "That's why it's so important to choose a partner whose character aligns with your values and beliefs from the start. It's easier to build a future together when you're walking in the same direction."

Tin-sing absorbed his father's wisdom, and after a moment, he ventured, "Have you and Mom faced challenges in your relationship?"

Menalik chuckled softly. "Oh, many, my son. Love is a journey filled with highs and lows. Your mother and I have had our share of disagreements and misunderstandings. But we've always come back to our shared values and faith to guide us through."

He continued, "You know, love isn't just about passion and romance. It's about commitment, understanding, and the willingness to weather life's storms together. It's about growing together, learning from each other, and being there for one another."

Tin-sing nodded, his heart filled with gratitude for his father's guidance. "Thanks, Dad. I'm learning so much."

Menalik smiled warmly. "You're welcome, Tin-sing. Remember, relationships are like that dance between your teeth and tongue—sometimes there'll be moments of discord, but when you work through them together, you'll find harmony and strength."

As the night settled in around them, father and son continued their walk, sharing not only the wisdom of generations but also the bond that would carry them through life's challenges, just as their teeth and tongue worked in tandem to navigate the complexities of living.

Love

In the warmth of a golden sunset, Menalik and Tin-sing settled on a park bench, a serene moment to discuss the complex and beautiful subject of love.

"Dad," Tin-sing began, "what is love, really?"

Menalik smiled, his eyes reflecting the wisdom of years. "Love, my son, is both simple and profound. It's a choice we make every day—a choice to embrace happiness, compassion, and understanding. It's not just a feeling; it's a conscious decision to care deeply for someone or something."

He continued, "Imagine love as a garden. When we tend to it with care, it flourishes, bearing fruits of joy, patience, tolerance, and forgiveness. But remember, Son, a garden needs constant attention and nurturing."

Tin-sing leaned forward, intrigued. "But what if we love someone, and they don't love us back?"

Menalik nodded, acknowledging the complexities of love. "Ah, unrequited love—it can be one of life's greatest tests. But love, my son, is not about what we receive in return. It's about the act of giving itself. When we give love without expecting it to be reciprocated, we free ourselves from disappointment and find a profound sense of fulfillment."

He shared a personal tale of love. "Once, I loved someone deeply, and my love went unanswered. It hurt, but in time, I realized that my love wasn't wasted. It had shaped me into a better person, one capable of greater compassion and understanding."

Tin-sing pondered this for a moment, then asked, "So, if we love without expecting love in return, are we giving something away, or are we gaining something?"

Menalik's eyes twinkled with understanding. "Both, my son. When we give love, we're not losing a part of ourselves; we're expanding our capacity for love. It's like a candle that can light countless others without diminishing its own flame."

As they watched children play nearby, Menalik continued, "And remember, love is not about possession. Just because you love someone doesn't mean they are obligated to love you back. Love freely, and in time, you'll find someone who appreciates and reciprocates your love. But until then, cherish the joy and growth that comes from giving love."

Tin-sing nodded, his heart lighter with understanding. "So, love is not just about finding the right person but also about being the right person."

Menalik patted his son's shoulder. "Exactly, Son. Love is a journey of self-discovery and growth. It's about becoming the best version of yourself and sharing that love with the world. In doing so, you'll find happiness beyond measure."

As the sun dipped below the horizon, father and son sat in comfortable silence, knowing that love, in all its forms, was a guiding force in their lives—a force that brought them closer to understanding the secrets of the heart.

Books

Menalik and Tin-sing found themselves seated on a park bench. It was a peaceful moment, the city's hustle and bustle fading into the background, as they delved into the world of books.

"Dad," Tin-sing began, "you've always had a love for books. What's so special about them?"

Menalik leaned back, a contented smile on his face. "Books, my son, are like windows to other worlds. They're the keys to unlocking knowledge, wisdom, and the experiences of countless people who have come before us."

He continued, "In this vast sea of literature, treasures are waiting to be discovered. But just as not all treasure is gold, not all books are worth your time. It's essential to select the best books first."

Tin-sing looked curious. "How do you know which books are the best, Dad?"

Menalik chuckled softly. "That's the beauty of it. There's no definitive list of the 'best' books because it depends on your interests, but I can share Six that have had a profound impact on my life."

With an air of reverence, Menalik began:

Hands down the best book is **The Holy Quran:** "When you read it, it's like having a conversation with Allah(SWT). It is a book that benefits you, it benefits your mind, your body, your heart, your soul, and your spirit. And it has everything, action, adventure, history, mystery, science, wonder, you name it, it is in there!"

2. "The Art of War" by Sun Tzu: "This ancient Chinese text isn't just about warfare; it's a guide to strategy and leadership. It teaches us about adapting to challenges and finding the path of least resistance in life."

3. "The Prophet" by Khalil Gibran: "Khalil Gibran's poetic masterpiece delves into life's most profound aspects. It's a reflection on love, marriage, work, and so much more. Each chapter is a gem of wisdom."

4. "The Book of Five Rings" by Miyamoto Musashi: "Musashi, a legendary swordsman, offers insights into strategy and self-discipline. His lessons on mastering one's craft can be applied to any area of life."

5. "Twenty Love Poems" by Pablo Neruda: "Love is a universal theme, my son. Neruda's poems are like love itself—tender, passionate, and boundless. They remind us of the depth of human emotion."

6. "The Gift" by Hafiz: "Hafiz's poetry is a celebration of life and the divine. His verses remind us of the beauty in existence, the joy of connection, and the importance of living in the present moment."

Tin-sing nodded, his curiosity piqued. "Those sound amazing, Dad. But there are so many books out there. How do you choose which ones to read?"

Menalik's eyes sparkled with wisdom. "You're right; there are countless books, and you can't read them all in one lifetime. That's why you should start with the best ones that resonate with your soul."

He leaned closer to his son, his voice filled with warmth. "Read not just for knowledge but for the way a book makes you feel. A great book can stir your emotions, challenge your beliefs, and open your mind to new perspectives."

As they sat there, father and son, under the watchful gaze of the moon, Menalik's words lingered in the air. The world of literature was vast and infinite, and with the guidance of these carefully chosen books, they were on the path to discovering its wonders.

Bad People

Menalik and Tin-sing sat beneath the shade of a great oak tree, the dappled sunlight filtering through the leaves as they shared stories, wisdom, and the kind of moments that bound hearts together.

Tin-sing's face bore the weight of a troubling question, one that had gnawed at his soul. "Dad," he began, "I've often heard people speak of 'bad people'—those who do terrible things. But is there such a thing as a truly 'bad person'? Can someone be so consumed by darkness that they are beyond redemption?"

Menalik's gaze turned thoughtful, and he reached for a small pebble at his feet. "You see this stone, Tin-sing?" he asked, holding it up for his son to see. "It's just like a person's heart. It can carry the weight of actions—good and bad."

He then set the pebble down and began to share a powerful truth. "There are no bad people, my son," Menalik said, his voice carrying the certainty of ages. "There are only bad actions. Remember, our Creator, in His infinite wisdom, did not grant us the authority to judge the essence of another's being. We are not the arbiters of a person's soul."

Tin-sing nodded, his heart aching with the weight of the lessons he was learning. "But what about those who commit unspeakable acts, those who hurt others without remorse?"

Menalik leaned in, his eyes full of compassion. "Indeed, there are those whose actions are heinous and cruel, and they must be held accountable for their deeds," he explained. "We may not like the actions they commit, and we may even be called upon to stand against them, to protect those they may harm."

As the words hung in the air, Menalik's gaze turned to a distant memory. "Let me share a tale with you, Tin-sing, one from the Native American teachings," he said, his voice softening.

He recounted the story of Onawa, the elder and grandmother in the Creek Nation, who had endured unimaginable suffering at the hands of white people.

In the heart of a serene, ancient forest, cradled by towering, ancient oaks and whispering pines, stood Onawa, a venerable elder of the Creek tribe. Her face, etched with the wisdom and sorrows of a lifetime, bore the serene grace of a grandmother who had walked through the raging storms of suffering. Her people revered her, not just for her age, but for the depth of her spirit, a spirit that had endured the crushing weight of grief and loss.

Many moons ago, Onawa's world had been shattered. White men, strangers to the land's sacred balance, had come like a relentless storm. They brought with them the thunder of guns and the lightning of cruelty. In a heart-wrenching night, under a starless sky, they had brutally taken the life of her beloved husband, a warrior of great courage and gentle heart. Her father, a sage and a guardian of tribal lore, had fallen too, his wisdom silenced forever.

The deepest cut, however, came when they tore away her daughter, Nila. Nila, the light of her life, with eyes as deep as the midnight sky and a laugh like the gentle rustle of leaves, was snatched from her loving embrace at the tender age of nine. Years later, tragedy struck again when Nila, brimming with the fire of her mother's spirit, tried to protect her young son, Chitto, from the same fate. Her resistance was met with merciless force, and she joined her ancestors, leaving young Chitto to face the world alone.

Chitto, now a young man of eighteen, had walked a path strewn with the harshness of prejudice and pain. Yet, the fires of resilience burned bright in his eyes. When he was finally reunited with Onawa, his joy was a tempest of relief and sorrow. "I hate White people," he declared with a voice trembling with rage and pain, "they are nothing but devils, and I will fight them until the day I die."

Onawa's eyes, pools of ancient sorrow, filled with tears. She shook her head gently, her gaze sweeping over her people, who had gathered around in a solemn circle. "My baby, my beloved grandson," she said, her voice a soft echo of enduring love, "you have experienced many horrors in your life by the white people, but I have experienced more, do you agree?"

A chorus of assent rose from the gathered tribe, a wave of shared grief and understanding.

Onawa continued, her voice steady yet filled with an ocean of compassion. "I don't hate the white people for what they have done to us. You cannot hate them for not knowing what they do is wrong. Grandson, they don't know what they are doing. If they truly knew the horror and the trauma that they are causing, they would not do what they are doing."

She paused, her eyes reflecting the wisdom of the ages. "Listen, when they wound us physically and emotionally, they wound themselves emotionally, mentally, but more importantly, spiritually. And spiritual wounds take a long time to heal. If they knew that, if they understood how long it takes for spiritual wounds to heal, they would not do what they are doing. So, I don't hate them. I feel sorry for them. They don't know. Now I am not saying don't fight them, I fought them my whole life right?" she asked

Another chorus of assent rose from the gathered tribe, affirming her lifetime of fighting and resistance.

Onawa continued "We have to fight. The Creator gave us two precious gifts, Life and Rights, and we must fight to protect those at all cost. But don't hate them, they truly don't know"

Her gaze then softened as she turned to the youngest members of the tribe. "Look at the little ones, the babies. When a baby goes near the cooking fire, we all rush to stop him because we know the baby will hurt himself. But the baby does not know that the fire will cause pain. And if the baby reaches the fire and burns himself, we don't hate the baby, nor do we punish him, because the baby did not know the pain it would feel."

As her words settled like gentle rain over the hearts of her people, tears flowed freely. They cried not just for the pains of the past, but in gratitude for the spiritual guidance and wisdom of Grandmother Elder Onawa, a beacon of hope and resilience in a world often clouded by sorrow and strife.

Tin-sing's eyes filled with understanding as he absorbed the wisdom of Onawa's words. Menalik continued, "Just as we protect a baby from the fire it doesn't understand, we must protect ourselves and others from harm. But we must never cross the line and label a person as 'bad.' We cannot fathom the depths of another's soul or the struggles they may be facing."

He then shifted his gaze to the heavens and shared another story, this time from the Islamic tradition—the story of a man who had killed ninety-nine people,. As Menalik recounted the tale of repentance and God's boundless mercy, Tin-sing listened with bated breath.

In a dry, desolate land, under a scorching sun, there was a man haunted by his past. He had caused the death of ninety-nine people, and his heart was heavy with regret.

Seeking forgiveness, he went to a local rabbi. The rabbi's home, filled with ancient books of wisdom, was on the edge of a busy town. The man, trembling with both fear and hope, asked, "I've taken ninety-nine lives. Can God forgive me?"

The rabbi, shocked and appalled, rejected him. "You've caused too much harm. God's mercy can't reach someone like you!" This harsh response crushed the man's hope, and in a moment of despair, he made the rabbi his hundredth victim.

Still, the man's desire for forgiveness didn't fade. He later sought advice from a respected religious scholar, who lived in a peaceful place surrounded by beautiful gardens. The man repeated his question. The scholar, understanding and kind, replied, "God's mercy is limitless. Nothing can stop His forgiveness if you're truly sorry."

The scholar advised him to move to a town where righteous people lived, to help him change his ways. Filled with new hope, the man set off on his journey. But fate had other plans, and he was on the brink of death during his journey.

At that moment, angels debated over his fate. Angels of mercy and punishment descended, each claiming his soul. The angels of punishment saw him as a sinner, while the angels of mercy recognized his genuine pursuit of redemption. To resolve this, the Arch-Angel Gabriel was summoned, to settle this dispute. He decided to measure the distance to the towns. If he was closer to the town of righteous people, he would be shown mercy.

A miraculous thing happened. God, in His infinite compassion, changed the earth's dimensions. The man was found closer to the town of righteous people.

Prophet Muhammad (Peace Be Upon Him) told this story, showing that the man was saved by God's mercy. This story teaches us about the power of forgiveness and the chance for redemption, no matter our past mistakes.

Tin-sing was moved by the story's profound lesson, and his eyes shone with newfound understanding. "So, even the darkest heart has the chance for redemption?" he asked.

Menalik nodded, his voice carrying the weight of this universal truth. "Yes, my son. No matter how dark the path, as long as there is breath in a person's body, there is the chance for them to return to God and be forgiven. We must pray for their guidance and hope that they find their way back to the light."

As they sat there, father and son, beneath the wise old oak tree, they carried with them the lessons of compassion, forgiveness, and the understanding that, in the grand tapestry of humanity, no one was beyond the reach of redemption.

Money

$\backsim\!\!\circlearrowleft\!\!\circlearrowleft\!\!\circlearrowright\!\!\sim$

The sun hung low in the sky as Menalik and Tin-sing found themselves by a quiet riverbank, the gentle sound of flowing water providing a soothing backdrop to their conversation. Today, the topic was money.

"Dad," Tin-sing began, "people often talk about money as if it's the key to happiness. Is it really?"

Menalik gazed out at the river, his eyes reflecting the wisdom of years gone by. "Make the money don't let the money make you. Money, my son, is a tool. It can open doors and provide comfort, but it's not the key to happiness. True wealth isn't measured by the size of your bank account but by the contentment in your heart."

He continued, "He who knows that he has enough is rich. It's about recognizing when you have all you need and finding joy in what you already possess."

Tin-sing listened intently, a spark of curiosity in his eyes. "You once told me that lending money can improve memory. How does that work?"

Menalik chuckled, recalling the earlier conversation. "Ah, the memory boost from lending money. It's quite simple, my boy. When you lend money, you create a bond of trust with someone. You're relying on your memory to keep track of the loan, the terms, and the repayment."

He explained, "It sharpens your memory because you have a vested interest in remembering the details. And as you help others by lending, you're not just aiding them financially; you're also helping yourself by exercising your mental faculties."

Tin-sing nodded, finding the concept intriguing. "So, it's like a win-win situation."

Menalik smiled warmly. "Indeed, my son. In life, it's essential to find those win-win situations, where your actions benefit both you and others. But remember, while money has its place, knowledge is the true wealth."

He looked at Tin-sing with earnestness. "Knowledge is better than wealth. You have to look after wealth, but knowledge looks after you. Wealth can come and go, but the knowledge you acquire stays with you, guiding your decisions and shaping your life."

As the sun dipped below the horizon, father and son sat in quiet contemplation. Money, they realized, was a tool to be used wisely, but true wealth lay in contentment, in the bonds of trust and memory, and in the enduring treasure trove of knowledge that enriched their lives.

Work

~~~~~~~

Menalik and Tin-sing found themselves in a bustling coffee shop, the aroma of freshly brewed coffee swirling around them. The topic of conversation had shifted to the world of work.

"Dad," Tin-sing asked, "what's the secret to success in your career?"

Menalik took a thoughtful sip of his coffee before answering. "Son, success in work, just like in life, often begins with a strong work ethic. It's about putting your heart and soul into what you do, treating every task, no matter how small, with diligence and respect. So it goes without saying that I am a big proponent of having your own company, being your own boss. You feel me? When you your own boss you make the rules. Win or lose it's all on you. A lot of people not ready for that and that's ok, because we all have to start somewhere and work our way up, for some it's working for someone else."

He continued, "When you're at work, work as if you're a slave so that no one can be your slave master. It's not about working to please others; it's about taking pride in your work and doing it to the best of your ability."

Tin-sing nodded, absorbing his father's words. "But what about forming friendships at work? I've heard people say it's essential to have friends in the workplace."

Menalik leaned forward, his expression serious. "Ah, the workplace friendships, Son, It's a tricky terrain. While it's natural to bond with colleagues, you must be cautious. In war, we take no prisoners, and in work, we take no friends."

Tin-sing looked puzzled. "Why is that, Dad?"

Menalik explained, "Workplace friendships can be a double-edged sword. While some may have your back, others may betray your trust. It's crucial to maintain a professional demeanor and not share too much of your personal life. Sometimes, people who seem like friends can lie or stab you in the back to get ahead in their careers."

He sighed, reflecting on his own experiences. "I've seen good people get hurt because they trusted their colleagues too much. It's not that you can't have friends at work, but you must be discerning about who you let into your inner circle."

Tin-sing took a moment to process his father's advice. "So, it's about finding a balance, right?"

Menalik smiled, his eyes filled with pride. "Exactly, my son. Balance is key in work and life. It's about working diligently, building your career, and forming genuine connections with those who share your values. But always remember that your primary loyalty is to yourself and your own growth."

As they finished their coffee, father and son, the weight of these work-related secrets settled in their hearts. Work was a realm filled with opportunities and challenges, and with Menalik's guidance, Tin-sing felt better prepared to navigate its complex landscape.

Addressing Unwanted Advances

Menalik had always believed in equipping his son, Tin-sing, with the wisdom to navigate life's complexities with grace and resilience. One sunny afternoon, as they sat on the porch, Menalik realized it was time to discuss a sensitive yet crucial topic: how to handle unwanted advances from people of all walks of life.

"Tin-sing," Menalik began, his voice gentle yet firm, "as you grow older, you'll encounter various situations where people might make advances that you're not comfortable with. It's essential to know how to respond respectfully but assertively."

Tin-sing, his curiosity piqued, leaned in attentively. "I'm listening, Dad."

Menalik began, "Sometimes, a friend might cross boundaries, making you uncomfortable. In such cases, communicate openly but kindly, expressing your feelings. A true friend will respect your boundaries."

"Unwanted advances can occur in professional settings," Menalik continued. "Politely, but firmly, make it clear that you're here for work or a professional relationship, not personal involvement. Document incidents and report them if necessary. One of the best ways to do this is to send the person an email especially a work email stating that you respect their feelings but you do not feel the same way and that you are only here to work and or that you would prefer to keep your relationship a professional one."

Tin-sing's brows furrowed. "What if it's someone higher up, like a boss?"

Menalik nodded. "In these situations, approach HR or a trusted higher-up if your boss is the problem. It's crucial not to compromise your well-being or values for the sake of professional advancement."

"Now, Tin-sing, there may be times when a complete stranger makes advances," Menalik said. "Your safety is paramount. Assertively but calmly make it clear you're not interested and maintain a safe distance. If you feel threatened, seek help immediately."

Tin-sing took in his father's words, understanding that assertiveness could help him maintain his boundaries while fostering respect. "And if someone doesn't respect my wishes?"

Menalik's expression grew serious. "If someone persists after you've clearly expressed your discomfort, disengage and remove yourself from the situation. Your safety and well-being come first."

He continued, "Remember, not addressing unwanted advances can lead to emotional distress, anxiety, and even danger. Trust your instincts and seek help if you ever feel unsafe."

Tin-sing nodded thoughtfully, absorbing the valuable lessons his father had shared. "Thanks, Dad. I'll keep this in mind."

As the sun dipped below the horizon, father and son shared a moment of quiet reflection, knowing that with the wisdom imparted that day, Tin-sing was better equipped to navigate the complexities of relationships and boundaries in a world where respect and assertiveness were the compass guiding his journey.

Defending Yourself

As the sun dipped below the horizon, Menalik and Tin-sing sat in the dimming twilight, their conversation taking a more serious turn—self-defense.

"Dad," Tin-sing began, "you've always told me that I must always be prepared to defend myself. Why is that so important?"

Menalik's eyes held a steely resolve as he responded. "My son, no matter who you are or who you become, you must always be prepared to defend yourself. Even the mightiest lion, the king of the beasts, protects himself against tiny flies."

He explained, "Life, my boy, is filled with challenges, and there will be times when you find yourself in situations where you need to stand up for yourself, protect your loved ones, and safeguard your well-being. It's not about seeking conflict but about being ready when it finds you."

Tin-sing absorbed his father's words, understanding the importance of self-defense in a world that wasn't always kind. "But how do I prepare for such situations, Dad?"

Menalik leaned forward, his voice steady. "Preparation, my son, begins with knowledge and awareness. Learn to recognize potential threats and avoid them when you can. Trust your instincts—they're a powerful defense mechanism."

He continued, "In physical self-defense, it's wise to train your body. Learn martial arts or self-defense techniques to protect yourself when needed.

Remember, the best defense is often to avoid danger, but when that's not possible, you must be capable of protecting yourself. So when someone starts talking loud and crazy, you know acting bananas, that's when you put on your monkey suit. See they are trying to act crazy to instill fear in you, because they know if a person becomes afraid then they are less likely to defend themselves when they are attacked. So remember monkey's eat bananas, when they get to acting crazy eat their ass up"

Tin-sing nodded, taking mental notes of his father's advice. "What about mental and emotional defense, Dad?"

Menalik smiled, proud of his son's insightful question. "Mental and emotional defense, my boy, are equally vital. Strengthen your mind through knowledge and resilience. In the face of adversity or criticism, be like a fortress—steadfast and unshaken."

He added, "And emotionally, never let the words or actions of others wound you deeply. Guard your heart, for it is your inner sanctuary. Just as a lion's hide protects it from flies, your emotional armor should shield you from hurtful words and negativity."

Tin-sing felt a sense of empowerment, knowing that he was gaining valuable insights into self-defense from his father. "Thank you, Dad. I'll remember these lessons."

Menalik placed a reassuring hand on Tin-sing's shoulder. "Remember, my son, it's not about seeking confrontation but being prepared when it finds you. It's about safeguarding yourself, your loved ones, and your dignity in a world that can sometimes be challenging. With knowledge, awareness, and the willingness to protect what matters most, you'll be well-prepared for life's inevitable trials."

As the stars began to twinkle overhead, father and son shared a silent moment of understanding, knowing that the lessons of self-defense would serve as a foundation for a resilient and empowered life.

Women

~~~ ❧❦❧ ~~~

Menalik knew that teaching his son, Tin-sing, about respecting and honoring women was a lesson that transcended generations. As they sat under the shade of a massive oak tree one serene evening, he felt it was the perfect time to pass down this essential wisdom.

"Tin-sing," Menalik began, his voice resonating with a profound reverence, "it's vital that you understand the importance of having a healthy and respectful relationship with women."

Tin-sing, eager to learn, nodded attentively. "I'm listening, Dad."

"Son," Menalik continued, "just as we honor and respect the Creator for bringing life into this world, women bear the incredible gift and responsibility of bringing forth life. It is a sacred duty, and I always honor and respect them for it."

Menalik gestured to the world around them. "Look at the world, Tin-sing. Women come in all ages, races, and social statuses. Each one carries a unique perspective and strength. I love, honor and respect this diversity."

"Remember," Menalik emphasized, "some women may not always respect themselves due to life's challenges or experiences. It's our duty to show empathy, not judgment. Lift them up with kindness and understanding."

"Support women in their pursuits and ambitions," Menalik continued. "They should have the same opportunities, respect, and rights as anyone else. Encourage and empower them to achieve their dreams."

Tin-sing absorbed his father's words, understanding that respecting women was not just a matter of courtesy; it was a deep-rooted reverence for the essence of life itself.

Menalik shared a personal story, his voice filled with emotion. "Son, I've seen the incredible strength of women in my life, from your grandmother to your mother. They've been my pillars of support and wisdom."

He continued, "By honoring and respecting women, you not only show your character but also show and honor your roots."

Tin-sing nodded, his heart filled with gratitude for the wisdom his father had imparted. "Thank you, Dad. I'll carry these lessons with me always."

As the sun set, father and son sat in silence, surrounded by the gentle sounds of nature, knowing that this lesson on respecting and honoring women would shape Tin-sing into a man who would inspire others to do the same.

Laughter

Tin-sing and Menalik strolled through the woods, surrounded by the whispering leaves and the symphony of birds. It was a day when the world seemed to be painted in vibrant colors, echoing the lessons that Menalik was about to share.

"Dad," Tin-sing began, "why is laughter so important?"

Menalik's eyes twinkled with the promise of a rich story. "Laughter, my son, is the heartbeat of joy, the rhythm of happiness, and the elixir of life. It's a force that can mend both body and spirit."

Menalik leaned against a tree trunk, his eyes sparkling with wisdom. "Let me share with you the profound healing power of laughter, Tin-sing," he began, "because it's not just one tale, but many that showcase its extraordinary effect."

"First, there's the story of Norman Cousins," Menalik explained. "He faced a grave illness, one that left doctors puzzled. But instead of succumbing to despair, he chose a path less traveled. Norman decided to immerse himself in the world of comedy. He watched funny movies and laughed heartily, discovering that laughter had an incredible ability to ease his pain and, over time, contribute to his healing. This tale reminds us that laughter, even in the darkest of moments, can be a beacon of hope."

He then continued, "Now, among Native American tribes, laughter is not just seen as entertainment but as a sacred medicine. They've long understood the profound connection between our physical and emotional well-being. Laughter, to them, is a potent elixir that can chase away not just illness but sorrow too. In the heart of their communities, storytelling often involves humor, ensuring that the healing power of laughter resonates through generations."

Menalik paused, emphasizing the importance of this topic. "There are two essential reasons why laughter is crucial, my son. First, it releases endorphins, the body's natural feel-good chemicals, which reduce pain and promote an overall sense of well-being. Second, laughter strengthens our social bonds, bringing people together in times of joy and adversity. In laughter, we find a universal language that transcends barriers, fostering connections and resilience."

With that, Menalik smiled warmly at Tin-sing, knowing that the gift of laughter was a treasure to cherish and share, a balm for the soul in times of hardship and a celebration in times of joy.

Menalik's eyes gleamed with the nostalgia of history. "In our history, son, laughter held a unique place among African American slaves. It was like a secret code, a lifeline, and it took the form of what they fondly called 'laughing barrels.' These barrels, my boy, were filled not with provisions, but with humor and hope."

He leaned in, eager to share this important piece of their heritage. "Inside those barrels, they stored stories passed down through generations, songs that resonated with the rhythm of their hearts, and jokes that defied the cruelty of their circumstances. They knew that even in the darkest of times, laughter could be their refuge, a brief respite from the weight of their chains."

Menalik couldn't help but smile. "And that, my dear son, is how the phrase 'a barrel of laughs' came into being. It wasn't just about the physical barrels, but about the enduring spirit of resilience and camaraderie. These barrels held the collective wisdom of a people who found solace in laughter."

"Now," Menalik continued, "let me share a couple of tales that highlight the importance of laughter in history."

"One of these stories comes from the life of Frederick Douglass," he began. "As you know, Douglass was born into slavery, but he managed to escape and became a prominent abolitionist. During his time as a slave, he witnessed unimaginable suffering. However, he also discovered that humor was a powerful tool against oppression. Douglass recalled that sometimes, amid the hardships, the slaves would engage in laughter. They'd tell funny stories or sing playful songs late at night when they thought their masters couldn't hear. It was their way of reclaiming their humanity and finding strength in unity."

Menalik took a moment to emphasize the significance of this history. "The effect of laughter in such dire circumstances was twofold. First, it provided a momentary escape from the harsh reality they faced. Laughter was a sanctuary where they could momentarily set aside their burdens. Second, it bound them together as a community. Shared laughter was a form of resistance, a declaration that despite their circumstances, they still had their spirits, their stories, and each other."

He then leaned in closer, as if sharing a secret. "Here's another remarkable story. Have you heard of the 'Chitlin' Circuit'? It was a collection of venues that welcomed Black entertainers during segregation. Performers like Louis Armstrong and Ella Fitzgerald graced these stages, but it was the stand-up comedians who often stole the show. They used humor to address the absurdity of racial discrimination and bring people together."

Menalik paused to let the significance of these stories sink in. "Son, the importance of laughter in our history cannot be overstated. It has been a means of survival, a weapon against oppression, and a bridge that connects us even in the most challenging times. Laughter's power lies in its ability to heal wounds, forge bonds, and remind us of our shared humanity."

Menalik's voice grew solemn. "But remember, Tin-sing, laughter is a force of light. Never use it to harm or hurt. Instead, use it to uplift, to bond, and to heal."

He added, "Laughter should be like a soothing balm, a reminder that in this world, where there's pain, there's also joy; where there's darkness, there's also light."

    As the sun filtered through the canopy, casting dancing shadows around them, father and son shared a moment of laughter. It was laughter born not from ridicule but from shared delight, a sound that resonated with the wisdom of ages. They knew that in a world often filled with strife, laughter was the gentle reminder that joy was always within reach, a precious treasure to be shared and cherished.

Gossip

Under the soft glow of the evening stars, Menalik and Tin-sing sat on the porch, the night air carrying their conversation to a weighty topic—gossip.

"Dad," Tin-sing ventured cautiously, "why is gossip such a poisonous thing?"

Menalik's eyes were serious as he began to unravel the intricacies of gossip. "Gossip, my son, is like a poison that has no antidote. It's a force that corrodes relationships, spreads falsehoods, and sows discord among friends and family. It can harm both the gossiper and the one being gossiped about."

Tin-sing nodded thoughtfully, aware of the destructive power of idle chatter. "But why do people engage in gossip, Dad?"

Menalik's voice carried a hint of sadness. "People, my boy, sometimes use gossip as a way to feel superior or to divert attention from their own flaws. They fail to realize that gossip not only tarnishes the reputation of others but also reflects poorly on the gossiper."

He continued, "Remember, no matter how big or small the gossip, even if you know it to be true, gossiping is the poison of relationships. It corrodes trust, erodes friendships, and creates divisions."

Tin-sing frowned, understanding the gravity of the situation. "So, how do we avoid being tainted by gossip, Dad?"

Menalik leaned forward, his eyes filled with wisdom. "First, my son, make a conscious choice to refrain from gossiping. Be mindful of the words you speak and the conversations you engage in. If someone tries to draw you into gossip, change the topic or remove yourself from the situation."

He added, "Second, always consider the source of the gossip. Is it coming from a place of honesty and goodwill, or is it intended to harm and create discord? Use discernment to judge the worth of the information."

Tin-sing listened intently, eager to learn how to navigate the treacherous waters of gossip. "And if we become the subject of gossip, Dad?"

Menalik's smile was reassuring. "If you find yourself in the crosshairs of gossip, my son, remember that your character speaks louder than any rumor. Stay true to your values, and trust that those who truly know you will see through the falsehoods."

He shared a personal story. "I once faced a situation where false rumors were spreading about me. It was a challenging time, but I chose to remain steadfast and let my actions speak for themselves. Eventually, the truth prevailed, and those who believed in me stood by my side."

As the night deepened, father and son contemplated the destructive nature of gossip and the importance of guarding their words and actions. It was a valuable lesson on the power of integrity and the need to rise above the poisonous whispers of idle chatter.

Friends

In the soft glow of a quiet evening, Menalik and Tin-sing turned their conversation to a topic that carried great weight—the importance of choosing friends wisely.

"Dad," Tin-sing began, "you've always told me to be careful about the friends I choose. Why is that so crucial?"

Menalik's eyes held gentle, fatherly wisdom as he spoke. "My son, the friends you choose will influence the course of your life. They are like the currents that steer a ship. Wise choices can lead to smooth sailing, while careless ones may lead to storms and shipwrecks."

He continued, "Imagine making friends with a pig, my boy. You may find yourself rolling in the mud. The company you keep has a profound impact on your character and your destiny."

Tin-sing nodded, contemplating the gravity of his father's words. "But how do I know who the right friends are, Dad?"

Menalik's voice carried the weight of experience. "True friends, my son, are those who stand by you not only in good times but also in bad. They are the ones who share your joys and sorrows, who lend a helping hand when you're in need."

He added, "A genuine friend is like a precious gem, rare and valuable. They lift you up, inspire you to be your best self, and support your dreams."

Tin-sing listened intently, eager to understand the qualities of a true friend.

"And what about friends who betray us, Dad?"

Menalik's expression softened with empathy. "Betrayal, my son, is a painful experience, and sadly, it can happen. But remember, it's a reflection of their character, not yours. It's a reminder to be discerning in your friendships and to choose those who share your values and principles."

He shared a personal story. "In my youth, I had a friend I trusted deeply, but he betrayed that trust. It was a difficult lesson, but it taught me the importance of being cautious in forming bonds and the need to value loyalty above all else."

As the night unfolded around them, father and son sat in contemplative silence, understanding that the friends they chose would shape their journeys. They knew that, like stars guiding a sailor through the night, true friends would illuminate their paths and lead them to safe harbors, even in the darkest of storms.

Children

On a warm, sun-kissed afternoon, Menalik and Tin-sing took a leisurely stroll through their neighborhood. Their conversation turned to a topic that had always been close to Menalik's heart—children.

"Dad," Tin-sing began, "you've often said that a child is like a cup. What do you mean by that?"

Menalik smiled warmly at his son's question. "A child is indeed like a cup. Just as a cup holds whatever you pour into it, a child will become what you nurture within them. It's our duty to fill their cups with knowledge, love, and values."

He continued, "You see, children are curious by nature. They're drawn to the world around them, eager to explore, question, and learn. It's like they have an insatiable thirst for knowledge and experiences."

Tin-sing nodded, recognizing the truth in his father's words. "So, Dad, how do we nurture and guide them properly?"

Menalik's eyes sparkled with wisdom. "To guide children, my son, we must first understand that they learn through observation and imitation. They watch our actions, hear our words, and absorb the energy of our environment."

He shared an anecdote. "I recall a time when you were just a toddler, and I watched you mimic my actions while playing with your toys. It reminded me that children learn not just from what we tell them but also from what we show them."

Tin-sing chuckled at the memory. "I used to love imitating you, Dad."

Menalik's voice softened with affection. "And it was in those moments that I realized the importance of being a positive role model for you, my son. Our actions, values, and the love we pour into their cups shape their character."

He added, "Remember, we should encourage their curiosity, answer their questions, and provide a safe space for them to explore the world. It's in that exploration that they develop their unique interests, talents, and passions."

As the sun dipped below the horizon, father and son continued their walk, the echoes of their conversation lingering in the evening air. They understood that nurturing and guiding children was a sacred responsibility, a journey of filling their cups with the wisdom, love, and values that would shape them into the best versions of themselves.

Internet

As Tin-sing grew older, Menalik knew that there were modern mysteries he needed to unravel for his son, mysteries that were woven into the fabric of the digital age. The father and son found themselves sitting in the warm glow of their study, surrounded by books and the soft hum of technology.

"Dad," Tin-sing began, his voice tinged with curiosity, "what's the Internet you know what is it really? Everyone at school talks about it."

Menalik smiled, adjusting his glasses. "The Internet, my son, is like a vast library that contains knowledge from all over the world. It's a place where people can share information, connect with friends, and learn about the world. You know a black man invented the internet? Philip Emeagwali, a math whiz who came up with the formula for allowing a large number of computers to communicate at once."

Tin-sing's eyes sparkled with interest. "That sounds amazing, Dad! Can I use it?"

Menalik nodded. "Yes, you can, but like any powerful tool, it must be used wisely. There are important lessons I want to share with you about the Internet."

With a sense of purpose, Menalik began his digital discourse. "First, remember that the Internet can be both a friend and a foe. It can connect you with wonderful people and ideas, but it can also be a place where your privacy can be invaded."

Tin-sing furrowed his brow. "What do you mean, Dad?"

Menalik leaned closer. "The information you share on the Internet, whether it's your thoughts, pictures, or personal details, can be like footprints in the sand. Even though you may outgrow them, they can remain visible for a long time. What you post today might affect your future."

Tin-sing looked thoughtful. "So, I should be careful about what I share?"

Menalik nodded. "Exactly, my son. Be mindful of what you post online. Protect your personal information, like your full name, address, and phone number. Don't share passwords with anyone, and be cautious about accepting friend requests from strangers."

Tin-sing listened intently, realizing the importance of Menalik's words. "What else should I know, Dad?"

Menalik continued, "Remember that kindness and respect should extend to the digital world too. Treat others online as you would in person, with empathy and understanding. Cyberbullying and hurtful comments can cause real pain."

Tin-sing took these lessons to heart. "And what about the things that are special and private, Dad?"

Menalik smiled, proud of his son's understanding. "Those, my dear Tin-sing, are the treasures of your soul. Just as in life, some moments and thoughts should remain between you and those you trust the most. Not everything needs to be shared with the world."

As father and son delved into the intricacies of the digital age, Menalik imparted wisdom that transcended the wires and screens. He knew that in the ever-evolving landscape of the Internet, the values of privacy, respect, and discernment would serve Tin-sing well as he ventured into the virtual world, forging his path while preserving the sanctity of his own identity and the dignity of others.

Kindness

As Menalik and Tin-sing continued their journey through the bustling city, the topic of their conversation turned to a virtue that had the power to transform lives—kindness.

"Dad," Tin-sing asked, "why is kindness so important? What does it really mean to be kind?"

Menalik, a beacon of wisdom, turned his gaze toward his son. "Kindness, my boy, is the gentlest of virtues. It's a language that transcends words, a force that has the power to heal wounds and mend broken hearts."

He continued, "To be kind means to treat everyone you meet with dignity and respect, regardless of their station in life. It means to offer a helping hand to those in need, to share a smile with a stranger, and to be the warmth in someone's darkest hour."

Tin-sing listened intently, absorbing his father's teachings. "But how do we incorporate kindness into our daily lives, Dad?"

Menalik's eyes gleamed with a soft light. "Kindness, my son, is not a grand gesture but a series of small, thoughtful actions. It's in holding the door for someone, in lending a listening ear to a friend in distress, and in saying 'please' and 'thank you.'"

He shared a story from his own life. "There was a time when a kind stranger helped me when I was in need. Their simple act of kindness left an indelible mark on my heart. It taught me that even in the busiest of lives, we can spare a moment to be kind."

Tin-sing smiled, appreciating the depth of his father's wisdom. "So, why is kindness so important, Dad?"

Menalik's voice resonated with warmth. "Kindness, my son, is the glue that binds humanity together. It's what makes the world a better place. It bridges gaps, mends fences, and brings solace to troubled souls."

He continued, "And remember, before you do anything, ask yourself two questions: 'Is this kind?' and 'How can I put more kindness into this?' Kindness, my boy, is a beacon that guides us through life's journey."

As the city's rhythm continued around them, father and son understood that kindness was not just a virtue but a way of life. They recognized that in every interaction, no matter how small, they had the power to infuse kindness into the world, creating ripples of positivity that would touch countless lives.

Charity

In the warm embrace of the city, Menalik and Tin-sing found themselves surrounded by people from all walks of life. The topic at hand was as universal as the air they breathed—charity.

"Dad," Tin-sing began, "what's the meaning of charity, and why is it important?"

Menalik gazed at his son with pride, knowing that this lesson transcended mere words. "Charity, my son, is a reflection of the goodness within us. It's the act of giving to those in need, driven by empathy, compassion, and a desire to make the world a better place."

He continued, "Charity is not just about handing over material possessions; it's about extending a helping hand, offering support, and sharing a piece of your heart with those less fortunate. It's a manifestation of love in its purest form."

Tin-sing listened attentively, sensing the profound significance of this act. "But, Dad, what's the difference between charity and giving?"

Menalik smiled, acknowledging his son's curiosity. "Charity, my boy, is a specific form of giving. While giving can encompass various acts, charity is giving with a purpose—to alleviate suffering, promote well-being, or create positive change. It's a deliberate act of kindness."

He elaborated, "When you give, you offer something willingly, whether it's your time, resources, or even a simple smile. And in return, you receive something intangible—the joy of knowing you've made a difference in someone's life."

Tin-sing nodded, absorbing the wisdom. "Tell me, Dad, what's the benefit of charity, aside from helping others?"

Menalik's eyes sparkled with understanding. "The benefits of charity, my son, are manifold. When you extend kindness to others, you not only bring comfort to those in need but also experience a profound sense of fulfillment and joy."

He continued, "Charity bridges the gap between individuals and communities, fostering a sense of unity and compassion. It's a reminder that we are all interconnected, and our actions can ripple through society, creating positive change."

As they continued their walk, father and son shared stories of their own charitable acts, the moments when they had witnessed the transformative power of giving. They realized that charity was not just about the material gifts but the human connection it forged—the unspoken language of souls that transcended words.

In the heart of the city, Menalik and Tin-sing found themselves surrounded by the tapestry of humanity, understanding that charity was not just an act; it was a way of life—a path to greater kindness, love, and shared humanity.

Giving

The sun was casting its golden glow over the city skyline as Menalik and Tin-sing sat in their favorite park. The topic of the day was giving.

"Dad," Tin-sing began, "what's the secret to giving? Why do some people seem to give from the heart, while others give reluctantly?"

Menalik took a moment to let the question sink in, his eyes fixed on a distant tree. "Giving, my son, is an art that goes beyond mere actions. It's about giving from the heart, regardless of what you offer—be it money, time, gifts, or even a simple smile. Souls have a hidden language, and they speak to each other when you give."

He continued, "Always remember, when you give, give from the heart, no matter what it is you give. That's why you can offer something small and seemingly insignificant, yet the receiver will appreciate it and love you for it until the end of days."

Tin-sing was captivated by his father's words. "So, when we give, we're connecting on a soul level?"

Menalik nodded with a warm smile. "Exactly, my boy. Giving is a profound way of connecting with others. It's about acknowledging their needs and offering a piece of yourself to make their lives better. When you give from the heart, you're not just providing material help; you're offering a piece of your soul."

"But, Dad," Tin-sing wondered, "how does giving benefit the giver?"

Menalik leaned forward, his eyes alive with the joy of giving. "Every time you give from the heart, you're not just helping others; you're healing a broken or damaged part of yourself. It's a soulful exchange where both the giver and the receiver are mended. In giving, you're filling your own heart with compassion, kindness, and love."

He continued, "Think of it this way: every act of giving is like a drop of water that cleanses your soul. Over time, these drops accumulate, and your soul becomes clearer and purer. So, the receiver isn't just benefiting from your gift; they're helping you on your journey of self-discovery and growth."

Tin-sing reflected on his father's words, his heart brimming with newfound understanding. "It's not just about what you give but how you give it, right, Dad?"

Menalik nodded, his eyes filled with pride. "Exactly, my son. Giving is a profound expression of love and compassion. It's a language that transcends words and speaks directly to the soul. And in the act of giving, we find not only joy but also healing, connection, and the purest form of human connection."

As they sat in the fading light of the day, father and son contemplated the beauty of giving. It was a lesson that touched the depths of their hearts, reminding them of the boundless capacity for love and kindness that resided within each soul.

Patience

Amidst the urban hustle and bustle, Menalik and Tin-sing found themselves immersed in a conversation about one of life's most essential virtues—patience.

"Dad," Tin-sing asked, "why is patience so important in life? What does it really mean to be patient?"

Menalik, the wellspring of wisdom, turned his gaze toward his son. "Patience, my boy, is the master key that unlocks many doors in life. It's the art of waiting, of enduring, and of keeping calm in the face of adversity."

He continued, "To be patient means to understand that everything has its time and place, and that rushing seldom leads to the best outcomes. It means to embrace life's rhythm, knowing that some things cannot be hurried."

Tin-sing nodded thoughtfully, absorbing his father's teachings. "But why is patience so crucial, Dad?"

Menalik's eyes held a serene wisdom. "Patience, my son, is the guardian of peace. It allows you to navigate life's challenges with grace and resilience. In times of uncertainty and frustration, it is patience that steadies the ship and guides it safely to shore."

He shared a story from their own lives. "Remember the time when we waited in that long line for hours just to get tickets to your favorite concert? Patience, my boy, turned a seemingly tedious wait into a memorable adventure."

Tin-sing smiled, recalling that day. "So, how do we cultivate patience in our lives, Dad?"

Menalik's voice was a gentle reassurance. "Patience, my son, is a virtue nurtured through practice. Begin by reminding yourself of its importance. When faced with a situation that tests your patience, take a deep breath and count to ten."

He offered further guidance. "Learn to embrace the present moment. Instead of dwelling on what might happen or what could have been, focus on what is. Patience thrives in the here and now."

As their conversation flowed, father and son realized that patience was not just a virtue but a valuable life skill. They understood that it could transform life's challenges into opportunities for growth and understanding. In a world that often moved at a frenetic pace, they recognized that patience was the compass that could guide them towards a more peaceful and fulfilling existence.

Poverty

As Menalik and Tin-sing continued their journey through life's lessons, they found themselves in a vibrant neighborhood filled with diverse faces and unique stories. Poverty, an ever-present companion in the world, was their topic of the day.

"Dad," Tin-sing asked, "how can someone maintain a positive outlook when they're faced with poverty and hardship?"

Menalik nodded, recognizing the importance of this question. "Tin-sing, my boy, poverty is a circumstance, not a definition of who you are. It may affect your external world, but it should never define your internal spirit."

He continued, "Imagine your teeth, Tin-sing. They never experience poverty, no matter what happens. They find a way to shine and play their role, ensuring your smile remains intact."

Tin-sing chuckled at the metaphor. "So, you're saying we should always find a reason to smile, even in tough times?"

Menalik smiled warmly. "Precisely. A smile is like a light in the darkness. It not only brightens your own spirit but can also bring hope and warmth to others."

He shared a verse from Hafiz: "Even after all this time, the sun never says to the earth, 'You owe me.' Look what happens with a love like that. It lights the whole sky."

Tin-sing took a moment to reflect. "So, it's about giving, even when you have little?"

Menalik nodded. "Exactly, my son. Giving, whether it's a smile, a kind word, or a helping hand, is a gesture of abundance from a heart that knows poverty is temporary. When you give, you remind yourself and others that you are more than your circumstances."

As they continued their walk, they noticed a street performer, juggling brightly colored balls while wearing a broad grin. Despite the meager crowd, the performer's joy was infectious.

Menalik pointed to the performer. "Look at that, Tin-sing. That performer is embracing the spirit of abundance. They find joy in their art, even if their earnings are modest. It's a powerful lesson."

Tin-sing watched in awe, taking in the vibrant display. "So, it's not about what you have, but how you choose to see it?"

Menalik patted his son's back. "Indeed, my boy. Your outlook on life, even in the face of poverty, defines your true wealth. When you can find reasons to smile and share your light with others, you become richer than any material possessions could ever make you."

They continued their walk, their hearts lifted by the realization that, in the midst of life's challenges, the true treasure was the radiant spirit that could shine through even the darkest of days.

Borrowing

As Menalik and Tin-sing continued their walk through the bustling city streets, the topic turned to a matter that often had a profound impact on people's lives—borrowing.

"Dad," Tin-sing inquired, "what's your take on borrowing money? Is it something to be cautious about?"

Menalik, his eyes reflecting years of experience, replied, "Borrowing, my son, is a double-edged sword. It can be a helpful tool or a dangerous trap, depending on how it's used."

He elaborated, "Taking a small loan when you need it can be like a bridge to help you cross a temporary gap in life. However, one must tread carefully, for a small loan can quickly grow into a heavy burden."

Tin-sing listened intently, eager to learn more. "How does a small loan turn into a heavy burden, Dad?"

Menalik painted a picture with his words. "Imagine you borrow a small sum, and it helps you through a rough patch. But if you're not vigilant, more loans might follow, each with its own set of repayments. Before you know it, you're weighed down by debt, and that debtor becomes an enemy—a relentless burden you must carry."

He continued, "It's crucial, my son, to assess your needs carefully before considering borrowing. Ask yourself if it's a necessity or a luxury. And remember, every borrowed dollar carries a responsibility to repay."

Tin-sing nodded, understanding the gravity of the matter. "So, what's the best approach to borrowing, Dad?"

Menalik's voice was filled with wisdom. "The best approach, Son, is the one my mother taught me when I was 14 years old. She used to say, *'Don't touch anything you can't pay for.'* I remember being frustrated and confused because I just wanted to borrow my friend's shirt or something. My momma would say, *'If you don't own it, if you can't buy it, if you can't earn the money to pay for it, then it is not meant for you. God doesn't mean for you to have that right now.'* Tin-sing, I was so upset until my mother said these words: *'Son, when you borrow anything—money, clothes, electronics—anything, you put yourself in debt. And being in debt often is a burden and causes undue stress. For example, let's say you borrow that shirt from your friend and something happens out of your control to that shirt. Now, you owe your friend a new shirt, but how are you going to replace the shirt when you couldn't afford it in the first place? Or, if you borrow money from a so-called friend and that friend starts talking down to you and treating you differently because they think they are better than you for having loaned you money. You may not think this would happen, but it does, all the time. And if you live long enough, you'll see it with your own eyes.'*"

He continued, "And she was right. The first time I saw it was about two months later. One of my friends, Tim, borrowed a boombox radio from another friend of mine, Jerry, for two hours. Tim and I listened to some music and returned the radio to Jerry. The next day, Jerry yelled at Tim in school, saying Tim broke his radio and that Tim needed to replace it. I was shocked because I was with Tim the whole time he had the radio. In fact, we were sitting on my porch, and we walked to Jerry's house and returned the radio, and it was fine. The first thing that popped into my head was what my mother had said. Tim was very worried and stressed. A couple of weeks later, I talked to Jerry about Tim being stressed, and Jerry laughed and said his radio wasn't broken; he was just saying that to get some cash from Tim. I was so upset, and I told my mom what happened. She said, *'See, son, I was trying to protect you from any of that. Borrowing can put you in a very bad situation.'*"

Menalik paused, looking into Tin-sing's eyes with a depth that conveyed years of lived wisdom. "You see, Tin-sing, borrowing, at its core, is about trust and responsibility. But it's also a dance with uncertainty. You step into an agreement, hoping both sides understand and respect it, yet there's always a risk. It's like walking a tightrope without a safety net."

He sighed softly, the memories vivid in his mind. "My mother's advice was about more than just avoiding debt. It was about self-reliance and understanding the true value of things. She wanted me to learn that the worth of something isn't just in its price tag, but also in the peace of mind it brings. When you rely on yourself, you don't just own your possessions; you own your choices, your actions, and their consequences."

Tin-sing, absorbing every word, asked, "But Dad, isn't it okay to ask for help sometimes?"

Menalik nodded, a gentle smile on his face. "Absolutely, Son. Asking for help is a strength, not a weakness. But there's a difference between seeking assistance and becoming reliant on others for things you can achieve yourself. When you do borrow, do it wisely. Borrow for necessity, not for luxury. Borrow with the intention and the means to return it. And most importantly, borrow with the understanding that relationships are more valuable than the thing borrowed."

"As for the situation with my friend Tim," Menalik continued, "it's a harsh lesson about trust and integrity. Jerry's actions were unjust, and it shows how easily borrowing can turn sour, even among friends. Always remember, Son, your word and your integrity are like gold. Guard them fiercely. Don't let the desire for something temporary tarnish something as priceless as your honor."

Tin-sing nodded solemnly, the weight of his father's words sinking in. "I understand, Dad. It's about being responsible and valuing what's truly important."

Menalik squeezed his son's shoulder affirmatively. "Exactly. And sometimes, the greatest wealth is found not in what we possess, but in what we wisely choose not to."

As they walked on, the conversation shifted, but the lesson remained, etched in Tin-sing's heart - a guiding beacon from a father's wisdom, shaped by the love and teachings of his mother, passed down through generations.

Loss

Amidst the ebb and flow of life's unpredictable tides, Menalik and Tin-sing walked the bustling streets of their city, delving into a subject that touched every heart—loss.

"Dad," Tin-sing inquired softly, "why do we have to experience loss? It's so painful."

Menalik nodded, understanding the weight of his son's question. "Loss, my son, is an inevitable part of the human experience. It reminds us of the fragility of life and the depths of our emotions. It's through loss that we learn to appreciate what we have and to cherish every moment."

He continued, "Loss comes in many forms—losing loved ones, opportunities, or even our sense of security. It's a storm that can shake our foundations, but it's also a teacher that guides us toward resilience and inner strength."

Tin-sing sighed, recalling moments of heartache in his young life. "But, Dad, how do we cope with loss? It feels like a wound that never truly heals."

Menalik placed a reassuring hand on his son's shoulder. "Coping with loss, my boy, is a journey—a journey through grief and pain, but also a journey toward healing and growth. It's essential to allow yourself to grieve, to feel the depths of your emotions without judgment."

He shared a personal story. "When I lost my father, I felt as if a part of me had crumbled. But as time passed, I realized that while the pain never truly vanishes, it transforms into a source of strength and resilience. Loss teaches us to carry the memories and lessons of those we've lost in our hearts."

As they continued their walk, they encountered people from all walks of life, each with their stories of loss and survival. Menalik and Tin-sing listened, understanding that loss was a universal thread that bound them all.

Menalik's voice was filled with wisdom as he continued, "Resilience in the face of loss, my son, is not about forgetting or pretending the pain doesn't exist. It's about honoring the past while embracing the present and looking toward the future with hope."

They strolled through a park, the gentle rustling of leaves reminding them of the ever-changing nature of life. Menalik and Tin-sing knew that loss was an inevitable companion on their journey, but it was also a catalyst for growth and a testament to the enduring human spirit.

In that shared moment, father and son found solace in the understanding that while loss was a painful part of life, it was also a source of wisdom, teaching them to appreciate every sunrise and find strength in the face of adversity.

Freedom

Menalik and Tin-sing found themselves in a lively park one sunny afternoon. Underneath the vibrant green canopy of swaying trees, they embarked on a conversation about freedom—a concept both elusive and profoundly personal.

"Dad," Tin-sing began, "what is freedom?"

Menalik looked out at the children playing, their laughter filling the air. "Freedom, my son, isn't just about external circumstances. It's a state of mind, a way of being that starts from within."

He continued, "Imagine it this way: you're in a room with four walls. The walls represent limitations, challenges, and even adversity. But freedom, Tin-sing, is the ability to dance, sing, and smile within those walls, undeterred by their presence."

Tin-sing raised an eyebrow. "So, you're saying we can be free even when we're facing difficulties?"

Menalik nodded. "Exactly. In fact, it's during challenging times that our inner freedom shines brightest. Hope, dreams, and laughter—they are the keys to unlocking the doors within ourselves."

He shared an inspiring story. "There was a man, Siddhartha, who discovered the secret of inner freedom. He left behind a life of privilege and embarked on a journey of self-discovery. Along the way, he faced hardships, but he never lost his inner freedom. He found it in the simplicity of life, in the wisdom of the river, and in the stillness of his own heart."

Tin-sing was captivated. "But what about dreams, Dad? How do they relate to freedom?"

Menalik's eyes sparkled with wisdom. "Dreams, my son, are the wings of our soul. They lift us above the constraints of reality and inspire us to reach for the stars. When we dream, we set our spirits free, and that freedom empowers us to pursue our aspirations, no matter the obstacles."

As they watched a kite soaring high in the sky, Menalik added, "And laughter, Tin-sing, is the music of freedom. It lightens our burdens, strengthens our spirits, and reminds us that, even in the face of adversity, we can choose joy."

Tin-sing contemplated this as they strolled through the park. "So, Dad, freedom isn't just about being unrestricted; it's about embracing hope, dreams, and laughter even in challenging situations?"

Menalik smiled, a gentle breeze rustling his hair. "Exactly, my boy. Freedom is a state of mind, and it's within our reach, no matter the circumstances. When you have hope, dream big, and find joy in laughter, you are truly free."

Their steps grew lighter, their hearts filled with the knowledge that, in the dance of life, freedom was not merely an external condition but a radiant flame within, waiting to be kindled.

Problems

~~~~~~~~~~

Menalik and Tin-sing's journey led them to a bustling marketplace, where people hurriedly moved about their business. Amid the lively atmosphere, the topic of the day was problems.

"Dad," Tin-sing asked, "how do you handle problems when they seem overwhelming?"

Menalik smiled, understanding the weight of this question. "Well, my boy, when life presents you with an enormous challenge, it can feel like trying to eat an elephant all at once. That's when you remember to take it one bite at a time."

Tin-sing chuckled, intrigued by the metaphor. "So, what's the first 'bite'?"

Menalik nodded. "The first bite is acceptance. Accept that the problem exists, and acknowledge your feelings about it. This step is like taking a fork and knife in hand, ready to start."

Tin-sing listened intently. "What's next?"

Menalik continued, "The second 'bite' is breaking the problem down into smaller, manageable parts. Just as you'd cut the elephant into pieces, you divide the challenge into smaller tasks. This makes it less intimidating."

Tin-sing pondered this. "So, it's like creating a plan of action?"

"Exactly," Menalik affirmed. "Now, let's move on to the third 'bite.' This one is about seeking help and advice. Just as you might ask others for help with a big meal, don't be afraid to reach out to others who can offer guidance or support."

Tin-sing nodded. "I see, so it's not about facing problems alone."

"No, it's not," Menalik agreed. "Now, the fourth 'bite' is taking action. Begin working on the smaller tasks you've identified. As you complete each one, you'll feel a sense of progress."

Tin-sing's eyes lit up. "It's like enjoying each bite of the elephant one at a time."

Menalik chuckled. "You've got it, my boy. And finally, the fifth 'bite' is perseverance. Problems can take time to solve, just as it takes time to eat an entire elephant. Stay committed, and remember that persistence pays off."

Tin-sing felt inspired by his father's words. "So, Dad, you're saying that even the biggest problems can be conquered step by step?"

Menalik placed a reassuring hand on Tin-sing's shoulder. "Indeed, my son. Life's challenges may seem daunting, but with patience, determination, and the willingness to break them into manageable pieces, you can overcome anything. Just as Santiago in 'The Alchemist' pursued his Personal Legend step by step, you too can follow your path, solving problems along the way."

As they continued their journey, the bustling marketplace no longer felt overwhelming. Menalik and Tin-sing carried with them the wisdom of tackling life's problems, one bite at a time, with a heart full of determination.

Anger

Menalik and Tin-sing continued their walk through the vibrant city streets. Today's topic was one that touched every soul: anger.

Tin-sing asked his father, "Dad, why do people get so angry sometimes? It feels like a storm inside."

Menalik nodded, understanding the weight of the emotion. "Anger, my son, is like a fierce storm that brews inside us. It can be overwhelming and destructive if not managed wisely."

Tin-sing frowned, recalling times when he felt his own temper flare. "What do we do when it feels like that storm is taking over?"

Menalik offered his son a knowing smile. "First, my boy, you must understand that anger, in itself, is not evil. It's a natural emotion, like rain, essential for growth. But, like a storm, when it rages uncontrollably, it can cause harm."

Tin-sing listened intently, eager to learn. "So, what's the key to handling it?"

Menalik began to explain, "The key lies in acknowledging anger when it arises, like recognizing dark clouds gathering in the sky. Once you acknowledge it, take a deep breath to calm the initial surge of emotion."

Tin-sing took a deep breath, feeling the importance of Menalik's words. "What's next?"

"Next," Menalik continued, "is choosing how to respond. Just as you can decide to take shelter from a storm or stand in the rain, you can choose how to channel your anger. Make a conscious choice to respond constructively."

Tin-sing nodded. "So, it's about not letting anger control us."

"Exactly," Menalik affirmed. "Now, let's talk about the limitations of anger. Anger can prompt action, but it rarely resolves an issue. It's like a raging river; it might carve a path, but it often leaves destruction in its wake."

Tin-sing contemplated this. "So, there's a better way to solve problems than through anger?"

Menalik smiled warmly. "Yes, my son. 'The Prophet' reminds us that anger can be like a cooking fire; it can heat a meal, but it can also burn it. Instead, learn to cool your anger with understanding, patience, and empathy."

Tin-sing felt a sense of clarity. "So, it's about turning anger into a tool for positive change?"

Menalik nodded approvingly. "Precisely. Use your anger as a source of energy to address the issue constructively. Just as Santiago in 'The Alchemist' transformed his journey into self-discovery, you too can transform your emotions into personal growth."

As they strolled through the bustling city streets, Menalik and Tin-sing carried with them a newfound understanding of anger as a natural force that could be harnessed for good. Like skilled sailors navigating a storm, they were better equipped to manage their emotions, choosing to channel them into positive change rather than destruction.

Police

As the sun dipped below the horizon, casting a warm glow over the world, Tin-sing sat with his father, Menalik, under the same ancient oak tree where they had shared countless lessons before. Today was different, though, for Tin-sing had a question that had long weighed on his mind.

"Dad," he began hesitantly, "I've noticed that you never talk about the police. Why is that?"

Menalik looked at his son, his gaze reflecting a mixture of memories and emotions. After a moment of thoughtful silence, he replied, "Son, I was always taught that if you don't have anything good to say about something, don't say anything at all. But I will share with you some of the methods I use to survive encounters with the police."

Tin-sing leaned in, his curiosity piqued. "Please, Dad, I want to know."

Menalik nodded and began his poignant lesson, every word heavy with the weight of experience. "First and foremost, son, I want you to remember that police officers, like all of us, are human beings. They have hopes, dreams, good days, bad days, and fears. Understanding this is the foundation of my approach."

"If I'm pulled over at night," Menalik explained, "the very first thing I do is turn on the overhead light inside the car. This allows the officers to see inside clearly. Then, I raise my hands or place them on the steering wheel. This helps alleviate some of their fears."

"I always talk to them with respect," Menalik continued. "Respect is a two-way street. By respecting them, I'm sending a signal that I expect the same in return."

Menalik's voice held a deep wisdom. "Son, it's essential to look them in the eyes when you talk to them. This not only shows you have nothing to hide but also makes it harder for them to treat you poorly. It's difficult to harm someone when you're looking them eye to eye."

He paused, "Looking into someone's eyes reminds you that they're human beings too and deserve a certain amount of respect under God."

"I keep my license and registration in the sun visor," Menalik shared, "not in the glove compartment. It minimizes sudden movements and any misunderstandings."

With a hint of modernity, Menalik added, "I equip my car with dash cams and a rear cam. It provides an unbiased account of the encounter."

"I don't joke, argue, or lie," Menalik stressed, his voice unwavering. "Not because I fear them, but because I'm trying to make it back home to you and the family."

His eyes conveyed the depth of his love. "Son, I want you to understand that it's not about submission or weakness. It's about ensuring that I return to my loved ones safe and sound. If, despite all my efforts, God decides otherwise, at least I know I did everything in my power to make it back home."

Tin-sing listened, his heart heavy yet enlightened. He understood that these lessons weren't just about survival; they were about navigating a complex world with wisdom, respect, and a deep commitment to love and family.

Knowledge

The sun hung low in the evening sky as Menalik and Tin-sing continued their thoughtful walk. Tonight, they delved into the depths of knowledge.

"Dad," Tin-sing began, "why is knowledge so important? It seems like people are always learning something new."

Menalik smiled, pleased by his son's curiosity. "Knowledge, my boy, is like a vast ocean. The more you explore, the deeper it becomes, and the richer your life becomes."

Tin-sing pondered this for a moment. "But isn't there a limit to what one person can learn in a lifetime?"

Menalik chuckled softly. "Indeed, there's a lifetime's worth of knowledge to acquire, but the key lies in the pursuit, not the destination. Just as the horizon is unreachable, it's the journey itself that brings meaning."

His father's words resonated with Tin-sing. "So, it's about the joy of learning?"

Menalik nodded. "Precisely. Learning is a lifelong adventure, my son. 'The Prophet' teaches us that knowledge is a garden. If it isn't cultivated, you can't harvest it."

Tin-sing liked that analogy. "And what about wisdom? How is it different from knowledge?"

"Wisdom," Menalik explained, "is the fruit of the garden. It's the application of knowledge, the ability to discern, and the sound judgment to make decisions."

Tin-sing furrowed his brow, wanting to understand better. "So, knowledge is having the tools, and wisdom is knowing how to use them?"

Menalik beamed with pride. "Exactly. Wisdom is the compass that guides your actions. It's the difference between knowing how to build a boat and steering it safely through turbulent waters."

As they continued their evening stroll, father and son reflected on the significance of knowledge and the wisdom to apply it. Tin-sing began to grasp that in this vast world of information, it wasn't about the sheer volume of knowledge but the quality of wisdom it could impart. With each step, they carried forward the age-old wisdom of 'The Prophet,' cherishing the journey of learning and the profound value of wisdom that accompanied it.

Hope

The moon had begun its ascent into the night sky as Menalik and Tin-sing arrived at the topic of hope. The world was a place of wonder, but it could also be a land of trials and tribulations. Hope, Menalik believed, was the North Star that guided them through the darkest hours.

"Dad," Tin-sing began, "why is hope so important? What makes it different from any other emotion?"

Menalik paused for a moment, gazing at the starry canvas above. "Hope, my son, is the ember that glows even when the world is cloaked in darkness. It's the belief that no matter how dire the situation, there's a flicker of possibility, a chance for something better."

Tin-sing nodded thoughtfully. "So, it's like a light in the dark?"

Menalik's eyes sparkled with pride. "Exactly. It's that tiny light that tells you to keep moving forward, to keep believing when everything else seems lost."

As they strolled through the quiet streets, Menalik recounted a powerful lesson from history. "You know, African Americans, your ancestors, were once slaves. They endured unimaginable hardships. Yet, they carried a flame of hope within them, even in the bleakest moments."

Tin-sing was intrigued. "How did they do that, Dad?"

"They never gave up," Menalik explained. "They might have given in to the harsh reality of their times, but they never surrendered hope. They sang songs of freedom, they whispered dreams of a better future to their children, and they believed in a day when they would be free."

Tin-sing's eyes widened. "That's incredible, Dad. They didn't give up even when things were so tough."

Menalik nodded, his voice full of emotion. "Indeed, my son. Hope is what fueled their resilience. It's what helped them rise above their circumstances and fight for a better tomorrow."

As they continued their journey, father and son contemplated the profound power of hope. They shared stories of individuals who had overcome immense challenges, guided by the North Star of hope. Tin-sing began to understand that hope wasn't merely a feeling; it was a force, a force that could move mountains, break chains, and transform lives.

The night was deep, but hope shone brighter than ever in their hearts. Menalik knew that as long as they held onto hope, they could conquer any challenge, overcome any obstacle, and embrace a future brimming with possibility.

Pain

The night was cool and serene as Menalik and Tin-sing ventured into the realm of pain. The stars above seemed to twinkle with a knowing wisdom, as if they too had witnessed the human journey through trials and tribulations.

"Dad," Tin-sing began, "why do we have to go through pain? Why can't life be without suffering?"

Menalik, with the weight of years and experiences, smiled gently. "Pain, my son, is a teacher. It's a mirror that reflects our deepest selves. Just as a diamond is formed under immense pressure, we, too, are shaped by the challenges we face."

Tin-sing furrowed his brows, intrigued yet perplexed. "But pain hurts, Dad. It's not something anyone would willingly choose."

Menalik nodded. "You're right, my boy. Pain can be excruciating. It can shake the very foundations of our being. But it's in those moments of profound discomfort that we often discover our true strength, resilience, and capacity for growth."

Tin-sing listened intently, eager to learn more. "Can you give me an example, Dad?"

Menalik gazed at his son, his eyes carrying the weight of memories. "I do you better I'll give you two, Every prince must go through pain in order to become a king, do you understand?"

"I think so, in order for the prince to be a king his father has to die and that is a great pain" said Tin-sing

"Thats exactly it my son and on a deeper level it means that pain is apart of life #2 Imagine a seed, buried deep within the earth. It's dark, cramped, and it must push through the soil to reach the light. This process is painful, but it's also the only way the seed can become a mighty tree."

Tin-sing nodded, starting to understand. "So, pain is like the struggle of the seed?"

"Exactly," Menalik affirmed. "It's in those moments of struggle that we discover our resilience, our ability to endure, and our capacity for growth. Pain reminds us that we're alive and that we have the power to overcome."

As they walked through the quiet streets, Menalik shared stories of individuals who had faced immense pain and emerged stronger, wiser, and more compassionate. He spoke of ordinary people who had transformed their suffering into a force for good, helping others on their own journeys.

Tin-sing's young heart swelled with a newfound understanding. He realized that pain, as challenging as it was, could also be a catalyst for growth and transformation. It could teach empathy, resilience, and the enduring power of the human spirit.

The night grew darker, but Menalik and Tin-sing carried with them the illumination of this profound lesson. They knew that as they faced life's inevitable trials and tribulations, they would do so with the wisdom that pain, although difficult, could also be a beacon guiding them towards greater strength and compassion.

Forgiveness

Underneath the vast canopy of stars, Menalik and Tin-sing delved into another crucial aspect of life – forgiveness.

"Dad," Tin-sing asked, "why is forgiveness so important?"

Menalik's gaze turned thoughtful as he replied, "Forgiveness, my son, is a gift we give ourselves. It's the balm that soothes our wounded souls and mends the fractures in our relationships. Holding onto grudges and anger is like carrying a heavy burden. It weighs us down, preventing us from moving forward."

Tin-sing pondered this for a moment. "But what if someone has hurt us deeply, Dad? Is it easy to forgive then?"

Menalik sighed softly. "Forgiveness isn't always easy, Tin-sing. Sometimes, it's a journey we must undertake, step by step. But it's essential, for when we forgive, we liberate ourselves from the chains of resentment and bitterness."

As they walked, Menalik shared stories of forgiveness, tales of individuals who had found the strength to pardon even the gravest of wrongs. He recounted the story of a man who had forgiven the person responsible for a tragic accident, finding peace and purpose in helping others. He spoke of nations torn by conflict that had chosen the path of reconciliation over revenge, setting an example for the world.

Tin-sing listened intently, realizing that forgiveness wasn't a sign of weakness but a testament to inner strength. It required courage and empathy, the ability to see beyond the hurt and recognize the humanity in others.

"Dad," Tin-sing said, "I want to learn how to forgive, even when it's difficult."

Menalik smiled warmly. "That's a noble aspiration, my son. Forgiveness doesn't mean condoning or forgetting the wrongs done to us; it means choosing to release the grip they have on our hearts. It means allowing ourselves to heal and grow."

As they continued their journey, father and son walked in the profound silence of understanding. The lessons of forgiveness were etched into Tin-sing's heart, a beacon of hope and healing in a world often scarred by pain and strife.

War

~~~~~~~~~

In the hushed streets of the city, Menalik and Tin-sing delved into a topic as old as humanity itself—war. The weight of history, the echoes of battles long fought, and the scars of generations past seemed to surround them.

"Dad," Tin-sing inquired, "why do people go to war? Isn't there a way to avoid it?"

Menalik sighed, for this was a topic fraught with complexity. "War, my son, is a shadow that has followed humanity since time immemorial. It's born from the darkest corners of our nature—greed, fear, and the thirst for power. While we must always strive for peace, it's crucial to understand that conflict, in some form, is inevitable."

Tin-sing listened intently, sensing that there was more wisdom to come.

Menalik continued, "Conflict takes many forms. It may not always manifest as physical war, but it can be present in our lives as disagreements, misunderstandings, or even the battles we face within ourselves."

"Are there ways to avoid war, then?" Tin-sing asked.

Menalik nodded. "Yes, my son. The first step is to prepare. Just as a lion protects itself against flies, we must learn to defend ourselves. This doesn't mean seeking conflict, but rather being ready to protect what is dear to us."

Tin-sing pondered this. "And what if war cannot be avoided?"

"In times of conflict, if you must go to war, don't play, fight to win" Menalik advised, "remember that war can take many forms, and not all battles are won through force. Sometimes, the most potent weapon is understanding. Seek to understand the root causes of conflict, and strive for resolution through dialogue, empathy, and diplomacy."

As they walked through the dimly lit streets, Menalik recounted stories of leaders who had chosen the path of peace, even in the face of great adversity. He shared tales of individuals who had bridged divides and sown the seeds of understanding, proving that conflict need not always end in bloodshed.

Tin-sing absorbed these stories, recognizing the profound wisdom in his father's words. He understood that while war might be a part of the human experience, the way one approached it and sought resolution could make all the difference.

With each step they took, Menalik and Tin-sing carried with them the knowledge that conflict, though inevitable, need not define their lives. They would be prepared, not just for self-defense but also armed with the tools of understanding and diplomacy, striving for peace in a world where war was often too familiar a companion.

Enemies

As the sun painted the evening sky in warm hues of orange and pink, Menalik and Tin-sing found themselves discussing a topic as old as humanity itself—enemies.

"Dad," Tin-sing began, "how do we recognize our enemies? And what should we do when we do?"

Menalik's eyes held a steady gaze as he contemplated the question. "Recognizing enemies, my son, requires a keen sense of discernment. An enemy may not always be someone who openly opposes you. It can be someone who harbors ill intentions, envy, or seeks to undermine your well-being."

He continued, "But remember this, a snake that you can see does not bite. It's often the hidden enemies, those who smile to your face while plotting against you, that pose the greatest threat."

Tin-sing nodded thoughtfully, absorbing his father's words. "So, what do we do when we identify an enemy?"

Menalik's voice took on a tone of resilience. "Facing enemies and conflicts is inevitable in life, my son. It's a part of our journey. However, we should strive to handle them with wisdom and grace."

He shared a personal anecdote. *"When they act like an A.. I mean butthole treat them like dodo.* Back when I was an Anesthesia Tech there was this Anesthesiologist who had a tendency to yell at Anesthesia Techs in a disrespectful way whenever he got stressed, well one day he yelled at me during a surgery for no reason. I knew his tendency so I was prepared for this. I pointed a finger at him and said 'Don't ever speak to like this again, infact don't ever speak to me period.' And I walked away. From that point on whenever the doctor came around I would leave. The doctor tried on several occasions to get back in my good graces to no avail. But through that challenge, I learned resilience, determination, and the importance of staying true to my principles. So like I said earlier when someone is acting like a butthole you treat them like dodo, how do you treat dodo? You avoid it, you stay away from it and you don't play with it."

Tin-sing leaned in, eager to hear more. "And what did you learn from that experience, Dad?"

Menalik's eyes twinkled with wisdom. "I learned that enemies can be our greatest teachers. They test our character, sharpen our resolve, and reveal our strengths and weaknesses. Instead of dwelling on the negativity, we should focus on the lessons and growth that come from adversity."

He continued, "And remember, my son, not all conflicts require confrontation. Some battles are best fought with patience, understanding, and by rising above the negativity."

As the stars began to emerge in the night sky, father and son found solace in their conversation about enemies. They understood that adversaries were an inevitable part of life's journey, and how they chose to navigate those challenges would define their character and strength.

Goals

~⚬⟨⚬⟩⚬~

Under the canopy of a star-studded night, Menalik and Tin-sing walked in silence. The weight of the subject they were about to explore hung in the air like the anticipation before a storm.

"Dad," Tin-sing finally broke the silence, "how do you achieve your goals?"

Menalik smiled and looked at his son. "Goals, my boy, are the stars we set our course by in the vast sea of life. They guide us, motivate us, and give our journey purpose. But achieving them, well, that's a matter of wisdom and persistence."

Tin-sing nodded, eager to soak in his father's wisdom.

"You see, Tin-sing," Menalik continued, "a roaring lion kills no game. Goals are like the prey that we seek to capture. If we approach them too loudly, too forcefully, they'll sense our presence and slip away."

"So, what should we do?" Tin-sing asked.

"We should pursue our goals quietly and methodically," Menalik explained. "Just as a lion stalks its prey with patience and precision, we too should move towards our objectives with careful steps. This doesn't mean we lack determination or passion; it means we understand that some goals require subtlety."

As they strolled, Menalik shared stories of great achievers who, like the silent lion, had pursued their dreams with determination, yet without unnecessary noise. He spoke of inventors, artists, and leaders who had allowed their actions to speak louder than their words.

Tin-sing listened, captivated by the tales of perseverance and dedication. He realized that achieving goals was not always about making the most noise or seeking the spotlight. Often, it was the quiet, relentless pursuit that bore the sweetest fruit.

"But, Dad," Tin-sing asked, "what if our goals are grand, like reaching for the stars?"

Menalik chuckled softly. "Even the stars, my son, shine quietly in the vastness of the universe. Remember, it's not the noise that defines their brilliance; it's their unwavering presence and the light they emit. So, aim high, dream big, and pursue your goals with the heart of a lion, but do it with grace and humility."

As they continued their walk, father and son felt a sense of purpose, knowing that their goals, like the stars above, were there to guide them. Tin-sing understood that achieving these goals required not only ambition but also the wisdom to pursue them quietly, like a lion on the hunt, ready to pounce when the time was right.

Respect

As Menalik and Tin-sing continued their journey under the moon's gentle glow, a new topic came into the spotlight – respect.

"Dad," Tin-sing inquired, "why is it so important to treat everyone with respect?"

Menalik paused and looked at his son, his eyes reflecting the wisdom of years. "Respect, my boy, is the currency of humanity. It's a measure of our character and a reflection of our values. Just as we wish to be treated with kindness and dignity, we must extend the same to others."

Tin-sing nodded, absorbing his father's words.

"You see," Menalik continued, "respect isn't reserved for those who have earned it; it should be freely given to every soul we encounter on our journey. Whether a person is rich or poor, young or old, their worth is not determined by external factors but by the inherent value of being human."

The night breeze rustled the leaves above them, as if nature itself affirmed Menalik's words.

"Tell me, Dad," Tin-sing asked, "how do we show respect in our daily lives?"

Menalik smiled. "We show respect through our actions, Tin-sing. It's in the way we listen when someone speaks, the way we offer a helping hand to those in need, and the way we greet each other with a smile. It's in treating the janitor with the same respect as the CEO, recognizing that titles and positions don't define a person's worth."

As they walked, Menalik shared stories of remarkable individuals he had encountered throughout his life – people who had shown extraordinary kindness and respect, often to those society had marginalized. He spoke of a teacher who had transformed the lives of underprivileged children, a stranger who had offered assistance to a stranded traveler, and countless small acts of compassion that had ripple effects on the world.

Tin-sing realized that respect wasn't just a passive concept; it was a force that could shape destinies and bridge divides. It was the foundation upon which understanding, empathy, and unity were built.

"Dad," Tin-sing said with conviction, "I want to be a person who treats everyone with respect."

Menalik beamed with pride. "That, my son, is a noble aspiration. Remember, in a world often filled with discord and division, it's acts of respect and kindness that can heal wounds and bring light to the darkest corners of our existence. Respect is the language of our shared humanity, and when we speak it fluently, we create a better world for all."

Death

As Menalik and Tin-sing ventured further into the tapestry of life's mysteries, they found themselves standing on the precipice of the most profound and enigmatic topic of all – death.

"Dad," Tin-sing began hesitantly, "why do we have to talk about something so…sad?"

Menalik placed a reassuring hand on his son's shoulder. "Because, my dear Tin-sing, death is not just an end; it's an intrinsic part of the journey. To understand life fully, we must also come to terms with its impermanence."

They sat under the shade of a great oak tree, its branches whispering secrets carried by the wind. Menalik's voice was gentle as he spoke. "Death, my son, is a river we will all eventually cross. It's a destination we'll reach one day, but it's also a reminder that every moment we have is precious."

. "But Dad, how do we deal with the pain of losing someone we love?"

Menalik nodded, his eyes reflecting the wisdom of ages. "Losing someone we love is never easy. It's a wound that takes time to heal, and sometimes, it leaves a scar. But it's also an opportunity to celebrate the beautiful tapestry of moments we shared with them."

He continued, "Death, my son, teaches us to appreciate life. It reminds us to express our love and gratitude to those we hold dear while they're still with us. It encourages us to live fully, to pursue our dreams, and to leave a legacy that outlasts our mortal existence."

As the sun dipped below the horizon, father and son contemplated the infinite cycle of life and death. They understood that death was not the end but a transition, a doorway to something beyond their comprehension. It was the cosmic dance where stars were born and galaxies faded away.

"Dad," Tin-sing said softly, "I want to live a meaningful life."

Menalik smiled, his eyes reflecting the light of a thousand stars. "Then, my son, live each day as if it were a precious jewel. Embrace your dreams, be kind and forgiving, cherish your loved ones, and leave the world a better place than you found it."

With that, they rose and continued their journey, walking hand in hand, guided by the knowledge that life and death were two sides of the same coin, each with its own purpose and beauty.

About the Author

Tony Pang, a remarkable African American author, is a beacon of hope and love in the literary world. Born in Mobile, Alabama, and deeply rooted in his mantra, "Healing Hearts with Hope," Tony's writings reflect his profound commitment to this Deen. A Marine and a Martial Artist, his discipline and dedication shine through not just in his professional pursuits but also in his personal passions. Whether it's a day spent fishing, where the joy is found even when the fish aren't biting, or an evening immersed in the soulful tunes of Bobby Blue Bland and BB King, Tony's zest for life is palpable.

Tony's literary contributions span genres like Nonfiction, Fiction, and Philosophy. His influences range from the poetic musings of Hafiz and Khalil Gibran to the thrilling narratives of Sidney Sheldon and Anne Rice. Among his notable works are "Anesthesia Technician Survival Guide" and "Healing Status," both of which have garnered significant acclaim, showcases his multifaceted personality.

In essence, Tony Pang is not just an author; he's a storyteller, a healer, and a beacon of hope. Dive into his world, and you'll find tales that heal, inspire, and resonate with the heart.

You can connect with me on:

🌐 https://www.mesaiglobal.com

Also by Tony Pang

Shadows of the Asasiyyin

https://www.mesaiglobal.com/product-page/shadows-of-the-asasiyyin-the-asasiyyin-chronicles-book-1

In the bustling streets and historic corridors of modern-day Detroit, FBI Special Agent Anastasia Asma'u, rooted deeply in logic and law, finds her understanding of reality upturned when a murder case drags her into the realm of the supernatural.

Taqwah Travels Jassasah's Cave

Did you think you've seen all the dangers that there are? That's what Ibraheem and Menalik thought too! They have to face fresh challenges and dangers as they leave behind their home and those they love. Why? Because Princess Zaria has given Ibraheem and Menalik a CHALLENGE!

Will they rise up to the challenge of this adventure? Little do they know, but they will need all their courage to face the most terrifying danger in the whole world if they want to save a friend and themselves. Can you guess what this danger is…?

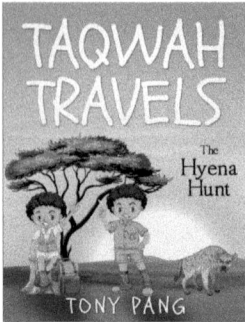

Taqwah Travels The Hyena Hunt

Did you think you had seen all the dangers that there are? That's what Ibraheem and Menalik thought too! But now they have to face fresh challenges and dangers as they leave behind their home and those they love. Why? Because Ibraheem and Menalik have been given a new CHALLENGE!

Will they rise to the challenge of this adventure? Little do they know, but they will also make new friends and allies. And some surprising enemies are waiting to harm them. Can you guess who they are…?

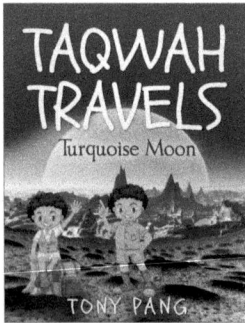

Taqwah Travels: The Turquoise Moon

Ibraheem was about to get really angry when he remembered all the trouble Menalik had caused with his challenge to fight a pirate. Suddenly Ibraheem laughed out loud. It was time for revenge. He looked at Menalik and grinned.

"I challenge you to catch a Firozian," he said gleefully.

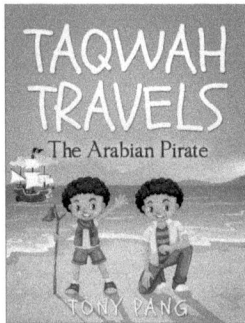

Taqwah Travels The Arabian Pirate

Did you think you've seen all the dangers that there are? That's what Ibraheem and Menalik thought, too! They must face fresh challenges and dangers as they leave behind their home and those they love. Why? Because Menalik has given Ibraheem a CHALLENGE!

Will Ibraheem rise to the challenge on this adventure? Little does he know, but he will also make new friends and allies. And some surprising enemies are waiting to ruin him. Can you guess who they are…?

Read on to see how your African-American Muslim heroes fare.

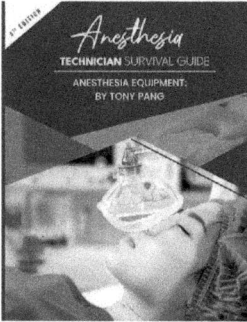

Anesthesia Technician Survival Guide 4th Edition: Anesthesia Equipment

The purpose of this anesthesia technician survival guide is to support the anesthesia technician as they continue their education and to help them better perform their duties in the operating room environment.